The Soldier

THE REVOLUTIONARY WAR SOLDIER AT SARATOGA

By William R. Sanford and Carl R. Green

Illustrations by George Martin

Edited by Jean Eggenschwiler
and Kate Nelson

PUBLISHED BY

Capstone Press

Mankato, MN, U.S.A.

Distributed By

⟨P CHILDRENS PRESS®
CHICAGO

CIP
LIBRARY OF CONGRESS CATALOGING IN
PUBLICATION DATA

William R. (William Reynolds). 1927-
The Revolutionary War soldier at Saratoga / by William R. Sanford,
Carl R. Green
p. cm.
Summary: Recreates the experiences of one soldier in the
Revolutionary War as he fights the decisive Saratoga Campaign.
ISBN 1-56065-000-1
1. Saratoga Campaign, 1777--Juvenile literature. 2. United Staes.
Continental Army--History--Juvenile literature. [1. Saratoga
Campaign, 1777. 2. United States--History--Revolution, 1775-
1783--Campaigns.] I. Green, Carl R. II. Title. III. Series: Sanford,
William R. (William Reynolds), 1927-   Soldier.
E241.S2S26 1989
973.3'33--dc20   89-25137 CIP AC

973.3
San

Illustrated by George Martin
Designed by Nathan Y. Jarvis & Associates, Inc.

Capstone Press
Box 669, Mankato, MN, U.S.A. 56001

CONTENTS

BEFORE THE BATTLE

Americans are a peaceful people, but they have often had to fight for their freedom. This tradition began in the early 1600's with the landing of the first colonists. Captain John Smith led the Jamestown colonists of Virginia in defense of their homes and farms. In Massachusetts, Captain Myles Standish organized the defense of the Plymouth colony. Skillful captains cannot win wars without brave men to follow them, however. As in every war, the burden of the fighting fell on the average soldier.

Americans fought beside British troops through most of the colonial period. That cooperation came to an end after the French and Indian War of 1763. Great Britain won the war, but the costs nearly emptied the treasury. Parliament took a hard look at the colonies and decided that they were not paying their fair share of the expenses. Laws were passed that put new taxes on the American colonies.

The colonists were outraged by the thought of paying higher taxes. Resistance came to a peak in Boston in 1773. A mob threw a ship's cargo of tea into the harbor rather than pay taxes on it. The British refused to overlook this illegal act. They closed the port and sent in an army to enforce the law.

The news of what was happening in Boston sent shock waves through the colonies. Many Americans picked up rifles and met on village greens to learn how to be soldiers. In New England, these citizen-soldiers formed **militia** companies called "minutemen." They were ready to take up arms at a minute's notice.

In April 1775, the British marched out of Boston, heading for Concord. Their goal was to capture the military supplies that the colonists had stored there. When the **redcoats** reached nearby Lexington, they found the minutemen waiting for them. The shots that were fired there signalled the start

Saratoga, New York, and the surrounding battle area.

of the Revolutionary War. On July 4, 1776, the new nation issued its Declaration of Independence.

The British generals planned a campaign that would split the colonies and win the war quickly. Three British armies were soon marching into New York state from different directions. Their goal was to link up with each other in Albany. If the Americans could not stop them, the Revolution would probably fail.

This slow-moving campaign ended late in 1777. In the fields outside Saratoga, the British and American armies prepared for a decisive battle. This was a fight the Americans had to win.

ELBERT PARTIN, RIFLEMAN

As soon as he woke up, Elbert Partin sniffed the air. He smelled bacon frying. Good, he thought. If the officers are giving us time to cook, it means the redcoats have not moved.

Elbert shivered and pulled his blanket tighter around his shoulders. Frost showed on the grass, even though it was only October 7. Winter had come early here in northern New York.

With a sigh, Elbert kicked free of his blanket. He stretched, then shook pine needles from his buckskin jacket. The cold cut through his fringed shirt and breeches. At least, Elbert thought, his worn buckskins were neatly patched. Some of the American troops were wearing uniforms that were little

9

more than rags. Quickly, he rolled up his blanket and tied it securely to his pack. He would not get another blanket if he lost this one.

As Elbert warmed his hands over a nearby campfire, he looked around. At twenty, he was one of the youngest of Morgan's riflemen. Even so, he felt like a veteran. He remembered that day in June of 1776 when he joined the company. Along with the other volunteers, he had ridden from Virginia to Boston to join General Washington's Continental Army. Six hundred miles in just twenty-one days! Who could have known then that Morgan's riflemen would become one of the army's best-known units?

In 1777, Washington had picked Morgan to lead a larger corps of riflemen. Elbert and the other Virginians were joined by hand-picked marksmen from Pennsylvania and Maryland. When the British invaded New York, the riflemen were sent to the Hudson Valley. They joined an army commanded by General Horatio Gates.

The Virginians were mostly Scotch-Irish, tall and lean. Elbert took pride in his own height. He had recently stopped growing at just over six feet. Americans seemed to be growing taller all the time. Maybe it had to do with their frontier way of life.

Someone at the next campfire started to sing, breaking the silence. The lively music and patriotic words of "Chester" always made Elbert's heart beat faster.

Let tyrants shake their iron rod,
And Slav'ry clank her galling chains.
We fear them not; we trust in God,
New England's God forever reigns.

As Elbert listened, his fingers traced the letters sewn on his shirt: Liberty or Death! He knew that Virginia's own Patrick Henry had meant it when he shouted that challenge. King George III had pushed them too far. Now, Americans were ready to rule themselves. That was what the Declaration of Independence was all about.

Like Elbert, the men around the fire were lost in their own thoughts. The word had moved quickly through the camp. The coming battle might be the most important since the **skirmish** at Lexington, two years earlier. After thirty months of fighting, they had a chance to destroy an entire British army.

As to the plans which had brought the two armies together, Elbert knew almost nothing. Soldiers followed orders and did not worry about strategy. At the moment, Elbert was more interested in breakfast.

THE BRITISH PLAN A QUICK VICTORY

Elbert hung his camp kettle over the fire and waited for the water to boil. His friends gathered around the fire, glad for a chance to warm their hands. Out of the corner of his eye Elbert saw Lieutenant Forbes walking toward them.

The men greeted Forbes with affection and respect. Like Colonel Morgan, he was a man they trusted. As they gathered around him, the lieutenant explained the British **three-fold plan**.

"Not far from here, as you know, lies one of three redcoat armies. Those are the troops of Gentleman Johnny Burgoyne." As he talked, Forbes drew his sword and scratched a crude map in the dirt. "Burgoyne's army moved south from Canada in the spring of 1777, heading for Albany," he said. "It was supposed to link up there with two other British forces.

"A second army entered New York from the west," Forbes went on. He pointed his sword at the spot. "This force, led by Colonel St. Leger, was supposed to sweep down the Mohawk Valley. Any Americans who tried to flee west from Burgoyne would have been trapped." The sword cut a path down the center of the map.

The men watched as Forbes pointed out a third spot on his map. "Finally, a third army under General Howe was supposed to move north from New York City," he explained. "If all went well, these three armies would have destroyed all of our forces in New York. At the same time, the New England colonies would have been cut off. Defeated and disorganized, the Americans would have to give up—or so the British believe."

"Their plan won't work, will it?" a soldier asked.

Lt. Forbes shook his head. "We have our work cut out for us," he said. "Burgoyne's army is large and well equipped. Gentleman

Johnny has over 3,700 British infantry and 3,000 hired Germans. He can also count on 150 French Canadians, 100 Tories, and 400 Indians. Along with their riflemen, the British can throw 138 cannon against us. They've dragged 42 cannons overland, and carried the rest on boats and canoes."

Elbert listened harder when the lieutenant began talking about the enemy general. "Burgoyne," Forbes said, "is both brave and capable. Remember, he's already captured his first target—Fort Ticonderoga. That's the fort that guards the route south from Canada. Our defenders slipped away without a fight when they saw British artillery on the high ground above the fort. That must have pleased Burgoyne! After that, he headed for Saratoga. If he wins here, he's only 30 miles from Albany."

"Did we let him advance without a fight?" Elbert asked.

"Our army didn't make it easy for him!" Forbes promised. "First, Burgoyne's men had to cross the wilderness between Lake Champlain and the Hudson River. American axmen chopped down trees and dammed creeks ahead of them. The redcoats must have thought they'd never get out of the back country. It took them four weeks to cover 20 miles."

The men smiled at the thought of the British sinking into hip-deep mud. Forbes replaced his sword and smoothed out the map with his boot. "When the redcoats finally reached the Hudson, they were worn out.

Also, there was some bad news waiting for Burgoyne. He learned that Howe's army was not coming north to meet them. Howe was moving south to attack Philadelphia."

"I heard that the news didn't worry Burgoyne," a young rifleman said.

"That's because Gentleman Johnny knew that his cannon and supplies were on the way," Forbes replied. "That left the British with one big problem. Because they were short of horses, some of their cavalry soldiers were walking. Burgoyne thought he knew how to get fresh horses, but he ran into a hornet's nest."

Elbert already knew that story. Burgoyne had sent raiders into Vermont, hoping to capture horses, wagons, oxen, and cattle. The plan fell apart at Bennington, Vermont. There, Americans led by John Stark surrounded the raiding party. Of the 800 Germans, Tories, and Indians, only nine escaped the trap. A British relief column bogged down in deep mud. Driven off by heavy fire, they never reached Bennington. The raid cost Burgoyne ten percent of his troops—and he never did get the livestock he needed.

A VICTORY AT
FREEMAN'S FARM

Caught up in the lieutenant's story, the men crowded in closer. "They look ready to fight," Elbert assured himself. "They're tough enough to beat the redcoats, that's for sure."

"Our victory at Bennington was good news, but that wasn't all," Forbes went on. "By then, Burgoyne knew he wasn't going to get any help from St. Leger. Benedict Arnold had led a relief force to help the garrison at Fort Stanwix. After St. Leger's Indian and Tory allies began to desert, he decided it was time to turn for home. Arnold let him go, happy to pick up the tents, ammunition, and supplies he left behind."

Forbes started to leave, but the men

demanded that he finish the story. The officer smiled at their eagerness. "Well, after that, Burgoyne didn't have much choice," he said. "He pushed on, trying to get to Albany before cold weather closed his supply line. After the British crossed to the west bank of the Hudson River, Burgoyne's scouts brought in more bad news. "Just south of his position, General Gates had fortified Bemis Heights. The fortress our boys built there was designed by Kosciuszko, the Polish engineer. Its log barriers and earthworks controlled the narrow plain beside the Hudson. In addition, the area in front of the heights was heavily wooded and broken by ravines. It was perfect country for American marksmen and hard going for the British."

Elbert thought about the battle that followed on September 19. When the British moved inland from the river, they met the American left wing at a place called Freeman's Farm. The battle surged back and forth across a wide clearing. The British held the field, but suffered heavy losses. More than 600 redcoats had been put out of action.

Every man in Gates's army knew what had come next. Instead of retreating, the British had dug in. Burgoyne's defense line now ran east from Freeman's Farm to the Hudson. His soldiers were protected by walls made of logs and dirt. Whenever they showed their heads, American **snipers** shot at them.

It was not only the snipers that kept British nerves on edge. Soldiers on picket duty never knew when they would be hit by an American raiding party. At night, packs of hungry wolves dug up graves and gnawed on decaying bodies. The cold wind whipped through British summer uniforms and food was running short. The threat of whippings and hangings had not kept some of the redcoats from deserting. But still Burgoyne held on.

Elbert ate his bread and bacon and thought about the coming battle. He knew he had been lucky so far. Sickness was common in the camp. Almost one man in five was ill. Many had come down with smallpox, and some of them were dying.

The possibility of falling ill or being wounded was a scary thought. Elbert remembered the day he had carried a wounded friend to the camp hospital. A doctor had to cut a bullet out of his back. The doctor had given his friend a ball of soft lead to bite on

during the operation. "Biting the bullet" was the only way to ease the pain. Medicines had to come from Europe, and the British navy had cut off the flow of supplies.

Elbert's friend had been lucky. Besides using a clean scalpel, the doctor had poured whiskey into the wound. These precautions had prevented infection. Elbert had helped bury seven men who had died in agony of infected wounds.

This was not the time to think about death, Elbert told himself. The stage was set for another battle. Faced by increasing numbers of Americans, Burgoyne had to attack. If he did not, he would have to turn around and return to Canada. Elbert hoped Burgoyne would make his decision soon. The Americans were ready for him.

THE REVOLUTIONARY SOLDIER AND HIS WEAPONS

After breakfast, a welcome sun drove away the chill. Elbert hurried to finish his camp chores. Although he might be facing the enemy soon, he was in a good frame of mind. Supplies were coming in from the other colonies. Better yet, more men were arriving every day. General Gates, the American commander, could count on almost 11,000 soldiers. Burgoyne, the reports said, now had fewer than 5,000.

No one wasted time this morning. Most of the men were cleaning their weapons. Elbert ran a cloth over the polished maple stock of his own Kentucky **flintlock rifle**. The metal fittings gleamed in the sunlight. The gun was one of a kind. Jacobus Scout, a well-known gunsmith, had made it for Elbert's older brother. Ernest had given him the gun when Elbert joined the army. He sighted along the eight-sided, five-foot-long barrel. "Watch out, redcoats," he whispered. He had seen the damage the gun's .60-calibre bullets could cause.

As he cleaned the grooved barrel, Elbert thought about the company's last target practice. He had put eight shots in a row through a 5-inch target at 60 yards! Colonel Morgan had praised him in front of the other men. Of course, most of them could match Elbert's shooting. On the frontier, poor marksmen went hungry.

Even though the Kentucky long rifle was accurate, it was not a perfect weapon. For one thing, it took a long time to load. Elbert cut a few more cloth patches and greased them. Whoever had come up with the idea of using the patches deserved a medal. Without the patches, a rifleman had to force the bullet down the barrel. That took precious seconds. Now, with the bullet wrapped in a patch, a few light taps with his ramrod did the job. The patch also held the round bullet snugly in place, cutting down on **misfires**.

Remembering his first battle, Elbert felt a little nervous. It took a cool head to reload while enemy rounds whizzed past. Shaking off the memory, he shook his own shot pouch. One of his friends had cast new bullets last night by pouring molten lead into a mold. Elbert guessed he had enough. It was time to load.

He kept his gun powder tightly capped in a powder horn. That was important, because wet powder would not fire. To make matters worse, the smelly black grains soaked up dampness like a sponge. He tipped the horn and poured some coarse powder down the barrel.

Next, he wrapped a bullet in a patch. Using his finger, he poked it part way down the barrel. Then he pushed the bullet to the back end of the barrel with his ramrod. He was careful not to tap too hard on the ramrod. One tap too many could set off a misfire. With the bullet seated, he snapped the ramrod into place under the barrel.

Still working quickly, Elbert opened the flashpan and half-cocked the trigger. Then he checked the touchhole, a small opening at the back of the barrel. The touchhole had to be kept clear. When clogged, it could cause a misfire called a flash in the pan.

From a smaller powder flask, Elbert sprinkled the flashpan with fine-grained powder. Practice had taught him to measure out just the right amount. Finally, he snapped the cover shut over the flashpan. At the same time, he tilted the gun and tapped it lightly to knock powder into the touchhole.

Elbert relaxed. From start to finish, he had loaded the rifle in only 20 seconds. If he pulled the hammer to full cock and took careful aim, he was sure he could hit a redcoat at 300 yards. Pulling the trigger caused the hammer and flint to snap against a steel plate. The resulting sparks entered the flash pan and ignited the powder there. The priming powder then sent a flash down the touchhole. This set off the main charge and fired the rifle. If he allowed for wind and aimed properly, the bullet would hit the mark.

Elbert imagined he had General Burgoyne in his sights. He steadied the long barrel and slowly squeezed the trigger. The rifle bucked and roared. Twigs exploded from a nearby tree. Everyone turned to look at Elbert, and someone laughed. He felt his face grow hot. Ducking his head, he started to reload.

Across the way, a group of soldiers in blue uniforms were drilling with muskets and bayonets. Elbert no longer sneered at their inaccurate smoothbore muskets. The three-foot barrels had only a quarter the range of his long rifle, but they could be reloaded and fired four times a minute.

Musket soldiers carried paper cartridges. To reload, they bit off the end of one and put a little powder in the pan. Then they poured the rest of the powder down the barrel. As soon as they rammed home the musket ball and wadded paper cartridge, the gun was ready to fire.

Besides, if the British got too close, the muskets carried sharp **bayonets**. That was something the longer, lighter rifles could not do. Riflemen had been forced to run more than once when British infantry broke into their lines. To counter that, General Washington had ordered Morgan's men to carry spears.

Now a better solution had been found. Morgan's riflemen were backed up by 200 men drawn from other units. Armed with muskets and bayonets, they defended the riflemen against the enemy's bayonet charges. Elbert sometimes laughed at their fancy blue uniforms. But he liked having them beside him during a battle.

A SOLDIER'S LIFE IS
NOT EASY

As Elbert reloaded, a huge man in buckskins walked by. Elbert and the other men jumped to their feet. Daniel Morgan was more than their commanding officer. He was a true hero. Elbert knew that Morgan had fought alongside the British in the French and Indian War. During that war, a British officer had hit Morgan with the flat of his sword during an argument. The angry American had turned and knocked the man down. As a result, Morgan's back still carried the marks of British punishment. Elbert had seen the deep scars left by the **cat-o'-nine-tails.**

Before he became a soldier, Morgan

had been a farmer and a gambler. He was a crack shot and he made quick decisions. Under his leadership, the unit always seemed to be in the right place at the right time. Elbert knew that the proud Virginians would never have followed a lesser man.

Elbert squinted at the sun. He guessed it was about eleven o'clock. The **pickets** over toward the British lines were still quiet. With little else to do, he thought about the back pay the army owed him. The states were always short of cash, so the men went unpaid for months at a time. When payday did come, the paper money they were given had little value. As a private, Elbert earned $6.67 a month. Artillerymen made $8.33, but Elbert preferred to stay a rifleman.

His stomach growled. Elbert wondered what they would have to eat for the noon meal. Each man was supposed to receive a pound of bread and a pound of raw meat each day. Once a week the supply crews handed out salt fish. When the supply wagons came on time, the men could expect milk, beer, beans, butter, and vinegar. But rations were often in short supply.

There was an answer to food shortages. In his spare time, Elbert often went hunting.

His last hunt had been a good one. Along with shooting two ducks, he had stolen honey from a wild beehive. Elbert and six of his friends combined their food and took turns cooking. Their iron camp kettle had turned out some hearty stews.

The thought of food made Elbert wish he had some money in his pocket. With a few coins, he could buy a meal from the women whose cookfires were burning nearby. These camp followers earned their way by cooking, sewing, washing, and nursing. Many of the women were wives and mothers whose homes had been destroyed. Staying with the army was the only life left to them.

Elbert looked over his equipment. If they were going to fight today, he had better be ready. After filling his tin canteen with water, he opened his deerskin knapsack. Inside were his drinking cup, hunting knife, wooden spoon, wooden plate, and hatchet. He had carved the cup, spoon, and plate himself. What he could not make was a tent. Sleeping in the open was not much fun during cold weather. When the army stayed in one place for a while, Elbert usually built a lean-to from tree limbs. After he plastered the limbs with mud and leaves, he had a snug shelter from rain and wind.

Elbert suddenly snapped to attention. "Come on, men!" an officer shouted. "It's time to move out."

The riflemen slung their packs over their shoulders and grabbed their guns.

Lunch would have to wait. Elbert stepped into the file of silent men without looking back.

In the distance, Elbert heard the sound of fifes and drums. He guessed the army was heading back toward Freeman's Farm. The smell of battle was in the air.

THE FIGHTING BEGINS AT BEMIS HEIGHTS

Elbert fell into step with the men ahead of him. The riflemen seemed eager for a fight, he thought. He knew it had not always been that way. In the early days of the war, they had often been outnumbered and outgunned. "But we were never outfought," the men always added.

Feelings of national pride had kept the army going. To be a Continental soldier, you had to believe in the new country. Otherwise, the dangers and hardships were not worth it. Some men had already quit and gone home to their farms and families.

Anger was another emotion that drove the army. Elbert shared the outrage that everyone felt over the killing of Jane McCrea. The story was still being told around the campfires. The beautiful young woman had lived near Fort Edward. She had been killed and scalped, the tale said, by an Indian from Burgoyne's army. Jane's boyfriend had seen her long, shining hair on a scalp in Burgoyne's camp. Despite this evidence, Burgoyne had refused to punish the killer. He feared the other Indians would desert if he did so.

Word of Jane's death flashed through the colonies. She had been a **Tory**, but the scalping stirred deep emotions. Thousands of shopkeepers, farmers, and seamen left their jobs to go against Burgoyne.

From somewhere ahead came the sound of a turkey gobble. Elbert reacted instantly, for it was Morgan's special signal. With the others, he slipped off the trail and formed a battle line in the trees. He looked down the slope and across a wheat field to the woods beyond. There were no redcoats in sight, but they could not be far away. His heart thumped in his chest. He gripped his rifle a little harder.

Sgt. Greene came down the line, whispering instructions. "Burgoyne's coming!"

he warned. "Our scouts say he's heading toward the high ground to our right. But he's only got 1,500 men with him. He left the rest of his force back at the river. Maybe he's just looking around, hoping we're asleep. If he shows up here, we'll give him what for! With Learned's regiments and Poor's brigade beside us, we outnumber the redcoats for a change."

Below Elbert, the wheatfield stirred in the breeze. A swarm of tiny black flies buzzed about his head. He shifted his position. Time passed slowly. Then, without warning, the first redcoats moved into sight on the far side of the field. The soldiers spread out in a long, thin line—and sat down. In a moment, the Americans saw the reason for their strange behavior. Work crews moved forward and began to harvest the ripe wheat!

Morgan's turkey call sounded again. The riflemen opened fire. Elbert's rifle bucked as he sighted and pulled the trigger. Some British soldiers dropped, but others raised their muskets and returned the fire. Their musket balls fell short of the Americans. Elbert fired twice more. Then he leaped up and ran forward with the others. They stopped when they reached musket range. The American muskets crashed out volley after volley, giving Elbert time to reload. The British lines seemed to melt away as the Americans pressed forward.

Elbert tripped and fell when he was halfway across the wheat field. A bullet tore off his hat. His eyes were stinging from the smoke and he was gasping for breath. Behind him, a wounded man cried for water. The smoke cleared a little and Elbert could see again. Just ahead, a British soldier stared up at him through the trampled wheat. His bayonet gleamed in the afternoon sun.

Where was his own knife? Elbert pulled his blade from its sheath. Then he took a deep breath and replaced his knife. The other man's eyes were fixed in a glassy stare. Elbert had seen that stare before. You learned about dead men in a war. This Britisher is no older than I am, he thought.

Heavy firing to the right caught Elbert's attention. General Poor's men were charging a line of British artillery. The brass cannon roared. Deadly **grapeshot** ripped gaps in the American ranks. Soldiers staggered and fell, but the blue uniforms could not be stopped. The British wavered, then fell back. The Americans swept over the British positions.

Behind him, Elbert heard a cheer go

up. A heroic figure on a chestnut horse swept out of the woods. Elbert waved his rifle and shouted with delight. General Arnold had taken command. Old Benedict Arnold himself! Rumors that Arnold had been asked to give up his command had recently swept the camp. The men had hoped the stories were not true. Arnold was a good man to have on your side during a fight.

Morgan called for another advance. Yelling like crazy men, the Americans charged the flank of the British 24th regiment. The British pulled back.

The riflemen pushed on. Minutes later, they came up against the British 24th again. General Simon Fraser had rallied his men. Elbert could see him, riding up and down the line, urging his soldiers on. Arnold had told Morgan that Fraser was worth a whole regiment. He had to be killed.

Morgan turned to his men. "That brave officer over there is General Fraser," he said sadly. "I admire him, but he must die. Do your duty."

Elbert squeezed off a shot that missed the moving target. As he reloaded, he watched Tim Murphy work his way up a nearby tree. Tim was an Indian fighter and a famous marksman. He would get the job done. Tim's first two shots grazed the general's horse. The third hit Fraser in the stomach. The wounded man held on tightly to the horse's mane for a moment. Seconds later, he slipped out of his saddle and fell to the ground. With his best general down, Burgoyne ordered a full retreat.

Arnold led the final attack against the British positions. As he advanced, Elbert came upon an American with his rifle raised. He was about to shoot a wounded British officer. Elbert grabbed the rifle. The soldier turned angrily, his mouth twisted with fury. Elbert looked closely at the thin young face. The boy could not have been more than fourteen years old. Elbert turned him around and sent him back to camp. The British officer gave Elbert a weak salute. Then he fainted.

Elbert trudged on, barely able to lift his feet. He gulped water from his canteen and wiped at a bloody gash on his arm. It hurt, but he could not remember how it had happened. Ahead, he saw General Arnold leading one last charge. Morgan's riflemen joined three other regiments in an attack on a log **redoubt**. This position was the anchor of the British right wing.

Arnold waved his sword as he rode his powerful horse into the redoubt. Elbert found the energy to break into a run. He wanted to see the end of this fight. When he reached the fort, he saw that the defenders had fled. Men were crowding around a figure who lay pinned beneath a wounded horse. It was General Arnold! His leg and thigh were crushed. Elbert pressed forward into the circle that gathered around the general. Arnold was barely conscious. He gave a final order before he passed out.

"No surgeon," the general whispered, "shall be allowed to cut off my leg."

As night fell, the size of the victory became clear. American losses were about 150, counting both killed and wounded. Burgoyne had lost over 600 men and most of his artillery. However, Burgoyne himself amazingly escaped serious injury. American riflemen had shot one horse out from under him. Other bullets had drilled holes in his hat and vest. But he had survived.

When Elbert rolled up in his blanket that night, the sights and sounds of battle filled his head. Too much blood, he thought, on both sides. Still, victory felt sweet. Above him, stars winked in the cold night sky.

The stars made Elbert think of the American flag, new that very spring. He smiled and dreamed about going home. Some day he would fly the Stars and Stripes over his own piece of land, he promised himself.

AFTER THE BATTLE

Elbert had good reason to feel content. The victories he helped win near Saratoga turned out to be the turning point in the Revolutionary War. When Burgoyne tried to retreat north to Fort Ticonderoga, he was slowed down by deep mud. General Gates followed him and the Americans were able to surround the British army. On October 15, 1777, Burgoyne surrendered.

The victory at Saratoga lifted the spirits of Americans starved for good news. Better still, Burgoyne's surrender convinced the French that they should enter the war against the British. King Louis XVI opened his ports to American ships only two days after news of Saratoga reached Paris. A treaty between France and the United States followed on February 6, 1778. Without French ships, men, and money, the Americans might not have won their Revolution.

After the Saratoga campaign, Morgan's corps of riflemen was broken up. The war dragged on until 1781, when the last major battle was fought in Virginia. Elbert was there, serving in a combined American and French army led by General Washington. After Washington trapped a British army at Yorktown, General Cornwallis surrendered. The defeat convinced the British that they should make peace. In 1783, officials from the United States and Great Britain signed the Treaty of Paris. The war was over.

As always, the kings and generals won their places in the history books. But Elbert Partin and countless other soldiers won the war. Marching, fighting, and sometimes dying, these men fought for the right to live as a free people. Elbert was luckier than most. He escaped both British bullets and the diseases that killed so many. After returning home, he became restless. He decided Virginia was too crowded. In 1785, he took his bride to Tennessee, where a new frontier was waiting.

America was growing. And Elbert Partin was ready to serve his country in peace as he had in war.

GLOSSARY

Key Historical Figures

GENERAL BENEDICT ARNOLD (1741-1801)—A popular American general who fought bravely at Saratoga. Two years later, Arnold turned traitor and sold military information to the British.

GENERAL JOHN BURGOYNE (1722-1792)—The British general who led his army to defeat at Saratoga in 1777. Burgoyne was known as "Gentleman Johnny" because he insisted on living well while he was campaigning.

GENERAL SIMON FRASER (1729-1777)—Brave British general who was shot at Bemis Heights while trying to rally his troops.

GENERAL HORATIO GATES (1727-1806)—The American general who commanded the Continental army at Saratoga.

KING GEORGE III (1738-1820)—The king of Great Britain during the Revolutionary War. King George helped cause the Revolution by trying to treat the American colonists as rebellious children.

PATRICK HENRY (1736-1799)—A Virginia patriot and orator whose speeches helped inspire the Revolution.

COLONEL DANIEL MORGAN (1736-1802)—An American frontiersman and soldier who won the affection and loyalty of the men he led.

GENERAL GEORGE WASHINGTON (1732-1799)— The commander-in-chief of the Continental army. Washington led the Americans to victory and later became the nation's first President.

Important Terms

BAYONET—A knife that fits on the muzzle end of a rifle. Soldiers use bayonets in hand-to-hand combat.

CAT-O'-NINE-TAILS—A whip that has nine knotted cords tied to a handle. It was named for the cat-like scratches it leaves on the skin of the person being whipped.

FLINTLOCK RIFLE—A rifle that fires when a flint snaps forward, producing a spark that ignites the charge.

GRAPESHOT—A cluster of small iron balls that is fired from a cannon. When fired, grapeshot spreads out like shotgun pellets.

MILITIA—Citizen-soldiers who are called to fight in an emergency but who are not part of the regular army.

MISFIRE—A gun that fails to fire properly because of damp powder, a poorly loaded bullet, or a flint that does not spark.

MUSKET—A smoothbore shoulder gun. Muskets did not have the range of long rifles, but they could be loaded faster.

PICKETS—Soldiers sent out on patrol as a way of guarding against an enemy attack.

REDCOATS—A slang term for British troops during the Revolutionary War.

REDOUBT—A small, fortified position, often used to strengthen a defensive line.

SKIRMISH—A minor battle between two small military forces.

SNIPER—A skilled marksman who fires on enemy soldiers from a hidden vantage point.

THREE-FOLD PLAN—A British plan to split the rebellious colonies by sending three armies to meet at Albany, New York. The plan failed because two of the forces turned back and Burgoyne's army was defeated at Saratoga.

TORY—An American who remained loyal to Great Britain during the Revolutionary War.